The Oxygen Man

The Oxygen Man

Joanne Limburg

To Antonella,

with best wishes,

Joanne Limburg

Five Leaves Publications
www.fiveleaves.co.uk

The Oxygen Man
by Joanne Limburg

Published in 2012 by
Five Leaves Publications,
PO Box 8786, Nottingham NG1 9AW
www.fiveleaves.co.uk

ISBN: 978 1 907869 58 7

Five Leaves acknowledges
financial support from
Arts Council England

Printed by Russell Press, Nottingham

Contents

Also by Joanne Limburg
Femenismo
Paraphernalia
The Woman who Thought Too Much

Sister

She will harrow this town, she will turn him up,
whole or in pieces. Being a sister,
she knows that brothers are born to trouble.
Her part is to rescue him,
lend him a heart to face his enemies,
or failing that, confound them herself
with withheld smiles, or with her sharp
big sister's tongue; and if she finds
them gone to ground, their damage done,
she'll cut the losses for both of them
and seek him out, wherever he's lying,
broken and say, *Brother, there's
no shame in one lost battle, or
in ten. Put the phial down –
don't drink!* And if it is too late
for that, she'll scruff the man and stick
her fingers down his throat, or find
an antidote, or make her own,
or heave time back, or failing that,
and even failing that, she'll take him home,
and never mind how small the pieces.

Brother

'Hi,' you said, whenever I picked up: your name
was never asked for. Of course I knew your name.

I can't unknow it now, and you can't make me.
I bagsied it, I chew on it; your name

is ever imminent on my tongue. I start
to talk about my son, but use your name

instead, run two names together just
like Dad would muddle ours — mynameyourname —

as if he had one composite child. Two 'J's,
two final 'n's — we nearly shared a name.

Now I'm Joanne, alone, and call your name.
For pity's sake, pick up.

Chaim

You tipped the liquid curse into your mouth
and knocked it back

    a father lifting his infant daughter
    caught the scent of bitter almonds

    a new PhD in his tasselled cap
    sipped champagne that burned his tongue

    the lager they served in the union bar
    was acrid, and it made him retch

    cycling up the Hill to school
    his hands blurred on the handlebars

    hand over hand, climbing the frame,
    a dizzy head, a failing grip

a baby boy named after life
lost consciousness, then nullified the word.

Welcome to the United States

Halfway to the home of the deceased,
I met a man with the softest voice in all Chicago

and offered him my passport (which,
to give some form to agony, I had almost bitten through).

He took it, and my mother's, apologised so sweetly
for the queue that I forgave him (but not America)

for being what he was. He had brown eyes,
and when he asked the purpose of our visit

and I explained, I thought they brimmed a bit,
like mine were brimming. I felt us

brim together, the soft-voiced man and I;
we were both of us bewildered, and so sorry

and we had to wonder, both of us, why someone
with a family would do a thing like that. His brother —

— well he was a junkie, missing for a month —
they found him when they dragged the lake —

so I was sorry now for his loss too, we were both
so sorry, and brimming together, and his fingers

were so deft and elegant as they tapped the keys, and how
warm, how tender his feeling heart under his uniform

as shyly, willingly, I ceded him my fingertips,
and offered up my eyes, and believe me, in that moment,

he could have taken everything, that soft-voiced man,
just to give some form to agony, that we might brim together.

From the Best Western, Kansas

From anywhere to here,
it takes a car.
Up and down the routes, they slice
the country into manageable portions.

Without a car,
it's unintelligible, edgeless:
send your mind to roam on foot,
you'll never get it back.

Minds or persons roam
at their own risk. It's no place
for walkers, with its scarcity
of pavements, its six-lane highways,

its clammy heat, that in the three steps
from the lobby to the car
that's taking you to breakfast,
can hug your breath away.

Your Lawn

Rabbits copy and paste themselves
across a lawn the size of an English churchyard.

Green light shrieks off imported grass,
bred to take the heat once dry,

now saturated from the reservoirs
they built to feed the sprinklers.

It's a lawn for looking at
and mowing. Not for stepping on:

along with shrieking light and rabbits,
it's a home to chiggers,

waiting to hop on board my pasty foreign legs
and burrow in, and itch.

You bought a ride-on mower,
admired your mown and sprinkled lawn

from the safety of the porch.
With all your care, and reservoirs,

the grass has taken well: you did your best,
though you weren't bred to take the heat.

Sylar and Elle

Into the midst of things more real
and personal, creep Sylar and Elle.
She is shaking with grief and rage;
he wants to know if he can feel

for someone else, he covets pain.
So he approaches her, this girl
whose father he scalped some episodes back,
and she cries *You!* and zaps him. And again.

I'll kill you! Zap! She hurls blue lightning
from her palms, it hits him dead
in the chest, and he falls back, his arms
spread wide, a T-shaped allusion to something —

make that 'someone' — the viewers know,
and maybe love, and maybe pray to.
Then, in case you hadn't got it,
he gets up. He has no wounds to show

but he looks chastened, and his shirt's
in charcoaled tatters. *I understand,*
he coos. *You hate me. Let me have it:
I can take it.* She slings her hurts

again. Again. The shirt is gone
completely. His body twitches back
to life, as we expect. He's keeping
calm. He's kept his trousers on.

Elle's given up, she's emptied
of her hate. His work complete,
Sylar crawls to her, the blue
sparks in his hands, all mended,

and they laugh. I never want
the scene to end, but it must.
I want to do what Elle does, give it
all to Sylar, but I can't.

Double Act

Straight away they clocked his face on me,
emerging from Arrivals on that unreal night,
crumpled, like a damaged photocopy,

the more disturbing for being almost right.
We had the usual laugh about it, how
they'd known me for his sister at first sight -

an old, familiar joke grown blacker now,
but still compelled to tell itself again
every time I smiled or raised an eyebrow.

All week I was the sick comedienne.
I did my accidental cabaret
for everyone who knew him, mixing pain

with mirth, as satirists always must. I'd play
the part according to the audience:
at breakfast, not quite Daddy; later in the day,

a young professor's echo; always a semblance,
never the real thing, a dreamer's version
of someone lost. I saved my best performance

for his memorial, a grand occasion,
catered, air-conditioned, floral. The crowd
itself, his colleague said, showed the impression

he'd made while he was there. We could be proud:
they hadn't had so many when Craig Venter
spoke. Posthumously, my brother wowed,

and so, accepting the honour as his sister,
I had to say, 'And I thought it was only
a career move for poets.' Laughter,

at this, was slight, and centre stage was lonely.

Night Flight

Nudging slowly into the dawn,
we have no choice. I'm in my seat;
above me in the locker, half
of what is left of you gets thrown

about like Duty Free. Nothing
can be done about this.
I'm sorry, sorry and afraid.
The clammy cabin air is something

I can neither scream nor sleep in.
When I try and watch a movie,
the engine's droning closes over
my ears. We're in a great tin

stomach, and it's digesting us,
noisily, a little every mile.
Here's a distraction at least: the sharp
wail of a toddler in distress,

a couple of rows behind, puke
down his pyjamas. So I think,
'Poor little guy, poor mother'.
I sympathise, I'm feeling sick

myself. The morning light is just
as green, shuffling in like a patient
returning obediently to bed,
where she'll wait quietly for breakfast:

good patients, like good passengers
never press the bell, not even
if they think they might be sick.
They never think to beg their keepers

to let them out, to let them go
right now, because whatever's outside,
dark or empty, it couldn't be worse:
the worst is here. That's all you know.

Notes to an Unwritten Eulogy

1. 'Da-Does': originally supposed to have been a corruption of 'Daddy', but subsequently discovered to mean 'my big sister'.

2. He never weed on her dress on purpose.

3. She only cut his blanket up into tiny pieces because she thought he'd agreed that she should.

4. Sometimes apparently ordinary children turn out to be the offspring of Dr Who, while the old lead-painted cot in their grandparents' box room is actually a Tardis.

5. 'Karate Man': a long-defunct superhero, costumed in a Mothercare dressing-gown.

6. 'Mrs P': although neither party could say what this signified, both understood it to be the worst thing you could possibly call a sister.

7. A 'marmite face' is the involuntary grimace made when a small quantity of salty yeast extract gets stuck between the upper lip and the gum.

8. By the time he outgrew her, he was already beating her at arm-wrestling every time, even when played left-handed.

9. Officially the funniest thing ever is the ping-pong ball that went pk-pk-pk-pk-pk all the way across the top of the radiator and then plonked onto the floor.

10. 'Rekop': a card game invented by the deceased. Similar to poker, except that players must hold their cards in such a way that their hands are visible only to their opponents.

11. 'The Clever One': a controversial title, best left unawarded.

12. The Yiddish proverb that made them laugh so much was: 'Your health comes first: you can always hang yourself later.'

13. Most likely potassium cyanide.

14. The winner is the child who still has a bit of Curly-Wurly left when their sibling has none.

Oxygen Man

Today, instead of dying,
you could go to work,
open up the lab
that has your name on it,

power something up —
some expensive toy
it took two grants to buy —
and set creation going.

I said *creation*. I know
the things that you can do:
engineer an enzyme,
speed up evolution;

one of your early tricks
was making oxygen.
Do that once more for me.
Take the manganese ions,

the ones the flowers use,
bind them up with ligands,
stick them in solution,
add your hypochlorite,

wait. We'll wait.
Maybe minutes, hours –
you know, I don't – but then
we'll see the bubbles rise.

Now that's your own good stuff:
breathe it, breathe it in.
Blue is not your colour.
Let everything be green.

Blue-Eyed Boy

Dying the way you did,
you reminded me
of how you used to cry,

how the blue would deepen
in your eyes, the apples
ripen in your cheeks,

your mouth release a wail
that couldn't be ignored,
as dismal weather broke

behind your baby lashes,
and when I picture it,
your blue gaze always latches

onto mine, glaring
shock and disappointment,
because I am your sister

and as such I should know,
but clearly don't, exactly
how to stop your tears.

The Door

Every day I stand
in the backwash of your silence,

witnessing your daily struggle
against the problem.

You see nothing else
and you deny me:

I'm only the living
and what can I do?

Only watch.
Only follow you

down the blind corridors,
trying not to lose you

as you flit from door to door,
rattle the handles, thump hard

with the flat of your hand,
trying to find the one that gives.

Proverbs 6:5-11

Perhaps you went to the ant
and considered her ways.
You watched;

she provided, she gathered —
meat and food, meat and food —
no guide or overseer,

no ruler, or apparent point.
All those hours
of meatless considering,

they tired you out,
didn't they? I think
you welcomed the hunter,

the fowler too,
I think you welcomed them
and folded your hands.

Not

When I lost my religion,
after a long wasting,
I felt as if I'd been
born again, and when

I say that I mean it was awful
to find myself thrown
naked to the world a second
time, to feel the terrible

rushing in of the real,
but not to have the means
of grabbing hold of it
and bringing it to heel,

and to have no more than snot
and shit and tears to use
to reach whatever's there.
If anything is. Now what?

On Holiday with Cotard

Honestly, the season's over. The sun's
its proper grudging self again,

the trees have given back their borrowed green,
flies are laying final clutches, and soon

they'll rest in spider-silk. Rest forever,
rest you well. Now it's time for everyone to relax,

the really thorough way, as you can when everything you fear
the most has happened already

and so you float on loose, float empty
just like the jellyfish, the moons and manes

that blister the sea on the Baltic Coast,
no longer pumping, and therefore not alive.

An Offering

A set of Trivial Pursuit, another of possible genes; a pear tree,
a tortoise, the ants in the garden; sick and silly jokes, a satellite
to bounce them seven hours ahead and back again.

The remote control, the microphone; the meaning and import
of certain remarks; the final word, the winning card; the truth
about who started what.

Superior height; Bar Mitzvah gifts, a tallis in a tallis bag; a
First, a PhD, a lab; a certain way with lucid dreams; a ride-on
mower, an early out.

Computer games on audiotape; copies of works by Stanislas
Lem; two Emu puppets, two Snoopy dolls; the very last time I
made you laugh; whatever you were thinking.

Ageing skin, stiffening joints; a slender orange vase from
Gumps; the joke about Dave who knew the Pope; one facetious
birthday card; however many years.

The Young Dead Poets

Lovely cop-outs,
they left us behind,
tidying up
in second-best bodies,

straightening backs
and grimacing,
then bending down
to tidy again,

depressing chairs
with leftover bodies,
deleting a line
then writing again,

straining not
to repeat ourselves,
repeating ourselves,
repeating ourselves —

forgive us, please
for repeating ourselves,
for being unlovely
and not copping out,

for staying behind
to tidy up,
to write, to fill
the graceless decades.

Notes

Proverbs 6:5–11

The relevant biblical passage is as follows:

5 Deliver thyself as a roe from the hand of the hunter, and as a bird from the hand of the fowler.

6 Go to the ant, thou sluggard; consider her ways, and be wise:

7 Which having no guide, overseer, or ruler,

8 Provideth her meat in the summer, and gathereth her food in the harvest.

9 How long wilt thou sleep, O sluggard? when wilt though arise out of thy sleep?

10 Yet a little sleep, a little slumber, a little folding of the hands to sleep;

11 So shall thy poverty come as one that travelleth, and thy want as an armed man.

On Holiday with Cotard

Cotard's syndrome is a rare neuropsychiatric disorder in which sufferers hold the delusional belief that they do not exist, are dead, putrefying, or missing some of their internal organs.

Acknowledgements

Acknowledgements are due to the editors of the following publications, in which some of these poems first appeared: *Poetry Salzburg Review*, *Magma*, *the Rialto*, *Tryst*, *Hearing Voices* and the Salt anthology *Contourlines*.

Poetry pamphlets from Five Leaves

Trailer
Anna Woodford
24 pages, 978 1 905512 31 7, £3.50

Willow Pattern
Penny Feinstein
39 pages, 978 1 905512 28 7, £4.50

By Heart — Uit Het Hoofd
Edited by Victoria Briggs
An English and Dutch poetry collection by Jan-Willem Anker, Maria
Barnas, Sarah Corbett, Antony Dunn, Daljit Nagra and Mustafa Stitou
32 pages, 1 9066512 22 8, £5.00

Tears of Honey and Gold
Jacqueline Karp
40 pages, 0 907123 55 4, £5.00

Flood Warning
Berta Freistadt
35 pages, 0 907123 94 5, £4.50

Choose Your Frog
Harold Rosen
35 pages, 0 907123 35 X, £4.50

The Last Hour of Sleep
Naomi Jaffa
32 pages, 0 907123 74 0, £4.75

Bed Time Reading
Adrian Buckner
23 pages, 978 1 907869 31 0, £3.00

Available from bookshops, or post-free from
www.fiveleaves.co.uk